DEAD MEN'S PRAISE

by Jacqueline Osherow

Jacqueline Osherow

April 7, 2005

Dear Lillian —

Thank you so much for having this. I hope there's something you like in here. I'm very grateful to you in deed.

yours
Jackie

Grove Press
New York

j.osherow@english.utah.edu

Published simultaneously in Canada
Printed in the United States of America

FIRST EDITION

Library of Congress Cataloging-in-Publication Data

Osherow, Jacqueline.
    Dead men's praise : poems / by Jacqueline Osherow.
        p. cm.
    ISBN 0-8021-3654-0
    1. Holocaust, Jewish (1939–1945) Poetry.   2. Jews Poetry.
  I. Title.
  PS3565.S545D4   1999
  811'.54—dc21   99-25483
                                                       CIP

DESIGN BY LAURA HAMMOND HOUGH

Grove Press
841 Broadway
New York, NY 10003

99 00 01 02   10 9 8 7 6 5 4 3 2 1

To the memory of my grandparents:

Dora Medvedev Osherow, Jacob Osherow,

Mollie Steiger Victor, Benjamin Victor

Contents

I

II

III

IV

Acknowledgments

"Ch'vil Schreiben a Poem auf Yiddish," *The Forward*
"Views of La Leggenda della Vera Croce," *Western Humanities
Review* and *Best American Poetry, 1998* (Scribner)
"Phantom Haiku/Silent Film," *Parnassus*
"Analfabeta," "Site of the Jewish Cemetery, Raciaz, Poland,"
Boulevard
"New Tanager/ New Song," *Literary Imagination*
"A Footnote for Perets Markish," *Seneca Review*
"One Last Terza Rima/ Italian Train," *Western Humanities
Review*
From "Scattered Psalms":
    I, VI, *Partisan Review*
    II, III, IV, *Triquarterly*
    V, XI, *Antioch Review*
    VII, *Solo*
    VIII, IX, *Paris Review*
    X, *The New Republic*
    XII, *Southwest Review*

The author gratefully acknowledges the help of the Guggenheim
Foundation, the Research Committee of the University of Utah,
and the Utah Arts Council. She is also indebted, yet again, to
George Bradley, Wayne Koestenbaum, and Barry Weller, for their
encouragement and attention to these poems, and to Saul Korewa,
for his help in reading and translating the Hebrew Psalms.

The dead don't praise God,

or the ones who go down to silence . . .

Psalm 115:17

I

Ch'vil Schreiben a Poem auf Yiddish

I want to write a poem in Yiddish
and not any poem, but the poem
I am longing to write,
a poem so Yiddish, it would not
be possible to translate,
except from, say, my bubbe's
Galizianer to my zayde's Litvak
and even then it would lose a little something,

though, of course, it's not the sort of poem
that relies on such trivialities, as,
for example, my knowing how to speak
its language—though, who knows?
Maybe I understand it perfectly;
maybe, in Yiddish, things aren't any clearer
than the mumbling of rain on cast-off leaves. . . .

Being pure poem, pure Yiddish poem,
my Yiddish poem is above such meditations,
as I, were I fluent in Yiddish,
would be above wasting my time
pouring out my heart in Goyish metaphors.

Even Yiddish doesn't have a word
for the greatness of my Yiddish poem,
a poem so exquisite that if Dante could rise from the dead
he would have to rend his clothes in mourning.
Oh, the drabness of his noisy,
futile little paradise
when it's compared with my Yiddish poem.

His poems? They're everywhere. A dime a dozen.
A photocopier can take them down in no time.
But my Yiddish poem can never be taken down,
not even by a pious scribe
who has fasted an entire year
to be pure enough to write my Yiddish poem,

which exists—doesn't he realize?—
in no realm at all
unless the dead still manage to dream dreams.

It's even a question
whether God Himself
can make out the text of my Yiddish poem.

If He can, He won't be happy.
He'll have to retract everything,
to re-create the universe
without banalities like *firmament* and *light*

but only out of words extracted
from the stingy tongues of strangers,
smuggled out in letters made of camels,

houses, eyes, to deafen
half a continent with argument
and exegesis, each refinement

purified in fire after
fire, singed almost beyond
recognition, but still
not quite consumed, not even
by the heat of my Yiddish poem.

Views of *La Leggenda della Vera Croce*

How will I ever get this in a poem,
When all I have to do is type AREZZO
And the name sidles up along a station platform,

The train I'm riding in begins to slow,
And—though I swore I wasn't getting off this time—
I know a train comes every hour or so

To wherever I'm headed—Perugia? Rome?—
And suddenly I'm rushing off the train,
Depositing my bag, crossing the waiting room,

And striding up the Via Monaco again
As if I couldn't see each fresco perfectly,
Couldn't see them, now, against this screen. . . .

But in a minute, they'll array themselves in front of me:
Soldiers, horses, placid ladies, kings,
All patient, in their places, not spinning crazily

Like the first time I saw them: unearthly beings
Breathing luminous pearl-green instead of air,
Horses and ladies-in-waiting flapping wings

Stolen from the eagle on the soldiers' banner,
Their brocaded sleeves and bridles grazing spinning walls,
Hats twirling, armor flying, coils of hair

Unraveling into whirling manes and tails—
And that was before the winged arm's appearance. . . .
When the *Times* ran an article about Stendhal's

Famous nervous breakdown from the art in Florence,
Half a dozen friends sent it to me.
I suppose these tales of mine require forbearance.

Not that I had a breakdown, though I was dizzy,
Closed my eyes, leaned against a wall,
And told myself that there was time to see

Each panel—one by one—down to each detail:
Hats, sleeves, daggers, saddles, bits of lace;
I studied every panel: *Adam's Burial,*

St. Helena's Discovery of the Cross,
Solomon Meeting Sheba, The Annunciation,
The Dream of Constantine, The Torture of Judas,

Whose other name I learned from a machine
Which, with the help of a hundred-lire coin,
Supplies a telephone with information.

I did it for a laugh; I chose Italian.
I thought I heard *the torture of the Jew*
And was so stunned I played the thing again

(My Italian was, after all, fairly new
And the woman on the tape spoke very quickly
But she did say *the torture of the Jew*—

In Italian it's *ebreo*—quite matter-of-factly)
The torture of the Jew who wouldn't reveal
The location of the true cross—I got it exactly—

Put in a lot of coins to catch each syllable
(I also heard the English, which said *Judas*),
All the while not looking at the rope, the well;

Instead, I chose a saintly woman's dress,
An angel's finger pointing to a dream,
A single riveting, incongruous face—

What was I supposed to do? They were sublime.
The Inquisition wasn't exactly news
And, while I did keep my eyes off that one frame,

I wasn't about to give up on those frescoes.
In fact, I saw them again, a short while after
And again soon after—in those heady days,

Trains cost almost nothing and a drifter
Could easily cover quite a bit of Italy,
Though I tended to stay in Tuscany. The light was softer,

And—probably not coincidentally—
It had a higher density than any other place
Of things that could dazzle inexhaustibly.

And I was insatiable, avaricious
For what—even asleep—a person can't see
From a slim back bedroom in a semidetached house

Like every other house in its vicinity
On a site whose inhabitants had been wiped out
To make room for spillover, like my family,

From the very continent I would have dreamed about
If I'd had even an inkling of the mastery
Of what its subtlest inhabitants had wrought

When they weren't doing away with people like me. . . .
See how Solomon, listening, leans his head?
How the tired horseman leans against a tree—

How the guard beside the emperor's makeshift bed
Can't resist the sorcery of sleep —
So only we can catch the angel's finger pointed

At the dreamer's head, the horse's sudden leap,
As if straight from that vision, to the battle scene:
Christianity's triumph over Europe. . . .

I love the wing, the arm, the dreaming Constantine,
The moonlight casting shadows on the tent —
It *is* moonlight, though there is no moon —

Pale, as always, silvery and slant;
It's coming from the angel's pointing arm
Which I didn't even notice that first moment —

All I saw was undiluted dream —
I didn't really care what it was for —
Besides, we fared no better under pagan Rome,

Which hadn't stopped me from going there —
I might not even have thought about Jerusalem,
If I hadn't found myself staring straight at her.

I was wandering lazily around the Forum
Without even a guidebook or a map.
I didn't care which stones were the gymnasium,

Which pillars hunched together, needing propping up,
Paid tribute to which boastful, scheming god.
Amazing, I suppose, that all that stuff could keep —

The advantage of stone, I guess, over mud and wood —
But the things I like best are always beautiful;
I don't admire antiquities as I should,

I lack the imagination for them. Still,
In my own haphazard way, I was thorough;
I did cover everything, though I'd had my fill,

Walked through every arch, every portico,
And—there—in the middle of the Roman Forum
Was my own first menorah, stolen years ago,

My altar, carved with rams' horns on its rim
(If you want to find them, they're on the Arch of Titus,
On your right, as you face the Colosseum;

Splendid reliefs, the *Blue Guide* says;
It's the only arch acknowledged with a star)—
Soldiers were parading them, victorious,

Transporting them—if only I knew where. . . .
What was I doing at these celebrations,
When I'd fasted over this, year after year,

Chanting the entire book of Lamentations
In candlelight, sitting on the floor?
How she's become as a widow, that was great among nations. . . .

The torture of the Jew couldn't compare.
After all, wasn't it a work of fiction?
This was actual footage from a war

Which had always been—forgive me—an abstraction,
Despite—or because of?—all the people killed
Trying to save the Temple from destruction,

The few survivors forced to watch as every field
Around Jerusalem was plowed with salt,
Then brought to Rome in chains, for all I knew to build

9

This very chronicle of their defeat.
Still, if you take the long view, here I am
And Titus isn't anywhere in sight.

Besides, I'd hate to sacrifice a ram
Or whatever's required—bullock, turtledove—
I much prefer the chance to chant a psalm

When I need a quick, relatively foolproof, salve
Or have managed to entangle myself yet again
In a muddle only God would ever forgive.

(Like this breeziness about the Temple's destruction,
This complete inability to feel its loss,
Not to mention my ridiculous and total passion

For Piero's *Legend of the True Cross*,
The way Jerusalem is most alive to me
When it looks just like Arezzo in his frescoes.)

It's not a matter of faith—though it should be—
But the chance to infiltrate with my own voice
All that unadulterated majesty.

Don't be too shocked, I'm often blasphemous;
It's a deal I have with God; at least I pray.
Though He may have a plan—I'm not impervious—

In which I'm expected to wake up one day,
Go to synagogue, recite the psalms,
And convince myself with every word I say.

Beggars can't be choosers; these are godless times;
Let Him hold on to His illusions.
Besides, maybe I do have a few qualms

About my persistent heretical allusions
To Someone who is — after all — a Deity. . . .
You'll find I'm a jumble of confusions.

Besides, I'm not sure God much cares for piety;
My guess is — since David was His favorite —
That He's partial to passion, spontaneity,

And likes a little genuine regret.
True, David lost his ill-begotten child —
But what did the pious ever get?

Unless you buy that dictum in the Talmud
That the reward for the commandment is the commandment —
In which case, nothing's ever withheld,

But that may not be what the rabbis meant.
And who am I, at the end of a mangled century,
To talk about God, reward, and punishment?

Especially from this vantage point, in Italy —
And that's where we are, gaping, in Arezzo —
Though there are lots of places we could be:

Florence, Santa Maria Novella, the piazza
Where they rounded up the Jews to ship them east . . .
Or reading some *well-known facts* about matzoh

In a just-published newspaper in Bucharest
(How it must contain the blood of Christian children);
Or even at a swim meet, as Europe's finest

Actually do a synchronized routine
About the Nazis and the Jews and win the cup.
Why not Ostia Antica, in the ruin

Of the oldest known synagogue in Europe?
Go yourself, take the Rome Metro, *Linea B*;
Otherwise, you'll think I'm making this up.

They found it building a road in 1960.
At first it looks like any Roman basilica:
Columns with ornate capitals, a stairway,

And then you notice bits of Judaica
On some of the columns — *lulav, etrog, shofar* —
And, after a while, looking down, the swastika

Patterned in the black-and-white mosaic floor —
I know, I know, it was an obvious design:
Bold, easy to lay out; you see it everywhere —

But to me, it's a harrowing premonition:
We should never have set foot on such a continent;
How could we have failed to see this omen,

Which, even in retrospect, will not look innocent
Of what it would inevitably mean?
As if no Jewish building on the continent —

Not even under layers of earth — escaped that sign,
But, still, it's third century (let's call it C.E.
Since *my* Lord is, after all, an older one)

And there — carved in the marble, for all to see —
Are a few of my most beloved eccentricities:
The *shofar*, with its desperate cacophony,

And the *etrog* and *lulav* — pure frivolities
Of gathered citron, willow, myrtle, palm,
Shaken in the air to jumbled melodies

Of a congregation belting out a psalm,
Then circling the room chanting hosanna.
Call it piety. Call it delirium—

Citron, willow, myrtle, palm, hosanna—
No one's even certain what they mean,
Unless it's sheer loveliness, sheer stamina—

Some say the citron's a heart, the palm branch, spine,
The willow leaf's two lips, the myrtle, eye
(Does every group of plants concoct a human?)

But this came after the commandment—some rabbi,
Improvising, finding similarities,
But I say God devised it purely whimsically—

(And ye shall take you . . . the fruit of goodly trees,
Branches of palm trees, and the boughs of thick
Trees and willows of the brook), merely to tease

The solemn air in which they were to frolic. . . .
Maybe God prefers synagogues as I do:
Dismantled, as in Ostia, bucolic,

A few columns and mosaics in a meadow,
The grass and weeds so high you think you're lost.
He can slip out, that way, incommunicado;

One day in seven isn't enough rest.
Not that I claim to understand His ways—
I'd fail, if He put me to a test

Of anything but willingness to praise—
But still, I would think the UJA
Or World Jewish Congress would be able to raise

Enough funds to pave a little pathway
From the rest of Ostia Antica to the synagogue. . . .
For older people, for instance, it's a long way

(Since, as usual, the local Roman demagogue
Banned synagogues within the city wall)
And some of them might be cheered to see an *etrog,*

A *lulav,* a *shofar* on an ancient capital,
The way, when I'm standing on the *bimah,*
Chanting ancient columns from a scroll

And come to, say, *They called the place Be'er Sheva*
And so we call it to this very day,
I feel a kind of wild reverse amnesia,

Having forgotten—and suddenly remembered—all eternity,
Proof, beneath my narrow silver pointer,
That there will be no end to this very day. . . .

But I'm forgetting the swastikas on the floor,
The distance from town, the torture of the Jew,
The roundup in Florence, the Judean war,

Who Italy's allies were in World War II
Before their final-hour about-face,
How—if you make your way to Urbino,

To enter the double turrets of the palace
That looks like something Piero once dreamed up
To house his enigmatic masterpiece

(*The Flagellation,* the reason for your trip)—
You will also have to forget the Paolo Uccello.
Or walk right by it. Don't even stop.

Don't let the helpful guide attempt to show
The beauty of its composition, frame by frame,
How the tiny golden circle that appears to glow

Between the stately woman's finger and thumb
Is the sacred host—stolen from the altar—
Purchased by a Jew for a hefty sum;

How the red stream, in the next frame, on the floor
Is blood from the host burning in his fireplace
As soldiers with spears and axes throng his door.

One child sobs, one grabs his mother's dress;
The blood has seeped outside, through stone and mortar
And into the next frame's version of the stateliness

Of a clerical procession to the altar:
Incense. Psalter. Cross. *The Host Returned.*
Next, the woman, out in a field somewhere,

Is met by an angel and . . . what? forgiven? warned?
Before the soldiers hang her from a tree. . . .
Then the Jew, with wife and children, is burned;

The flames near one child's head, the other's knee
(All four are tied together to the stake).
But we don't see the Christian woman die;

In the final frame she's on a catafalque,
A pair of devils grabbing at her feet
For what the angels, at her head, will not forsake

Without at least putting up a fight.
(My money's on the angels, but it's close.)
The guide calls it Uccello's greatest insight

To leave us with something so ambiguous—
A spiritual struggle . . . iniquity.
You see, I didn't heed my own advice;

I actually asked the guide to tell the story,
And a crowd gathered round to listen in.
No one blinked an eyelash but me. . . .

Perhaps they didn't notice the children
Burning, in that fifth frame, at the stake. . . .
It is, after all, a nighttime scene;

The Jew is wearing red, the children, black.
Besides, in Europe, burning Jewish children
Aren't all that difficult to overlook,

What with the complex struggle over sin
And so much never-ending beauty—
And even I, who see them, still take in

The two Pieros, the Raphael, the ideal city
Which unreal Urbino still resembles. . . .
Is there anything more despicable than ambiguity?

How could I not have left the palace in shambles?
Or, at least, burned the painting publicly?
I'm not interested in symbols

With two breathing boys right in front of me
Burning with their parents on a palace wall
For anyone who comes along to see

Or, rather, not see—since they're invisible
To all but specially trained eyes.
Tie a rope around me. Throw me in a well;

I'm sick of this unnatural disguise.
Sick of turning away. Sick of everything.
I need—as in Arezzo—to close my eyes,

To stop these flames and likenesses from spinning
From the painted to the identical real landscape,
But it's worse with my eyes closed; now they're careening

Around my tight-shut eyelids' burning map—
That red you get when you shut your eyes in sunlight
Consuming the entire extent of Europe—

A continent notoriously profligate
Of knees, heads, fingers, elbows, thighs.
Wasn't *this* Uccello's greatest insight:

That if you gradually habituate the eyes
They will be capable of watching anything?
I wonder if this came to God as a surprise.

Could He actually have known about this failing
And still gone ahead with our creation?
You can't, after all, have everything;

We're pretty good at visual representation,
Not to mention all those people who could sing
And care for sheep while arguing with a vision. . . .

He's certainly done His share of watching
And nonetheless managed to survive.
Unless He hasn't. But I'm not touching

That one. Besides, when you work out how to live
Your one puny life on this unnerving earth,
It's so much more appealing to believe

In some strategic artistry, some worth,
As if bitterness were a fleeting misconception.
I do have a fondness for the truth

But am willing to make, in this case, an exception,
Which has been, more or less, my people's way.
We've learned to be remarkable at self-deception

What with the Messiah's long delay. . . .
Just look at the Jew in the fresco in Arezzo,
Why have I avoided him until today?

Clearly he's faking it—the first Marrano
(According to the legend he's accepting Jesus)—
That's not how rapture looks to Piero;

The over-the-top bliss is preposterous.
The Jew was probably desperate to get dry. . . .
He hasn't got a clue about the location of the cross;

He can't even manage his own inventory.
Where's his holy ark? his candelabrum?
Why are these bits of ash dredging the sky?

Where's his citron, willow, myrtle, palm?
What's that splinter in his upturned eye?

II

Phantom Haiku/Silent Film

*Friends part
forever—wild geese
lost in cloud*
                Bashō

I don't write haiku. I'm no good at silence,
 Which may be why I crave those movies so much,
Though someone told me it's the silver nitrate,
The way it so luxuriates in light
That anything relinquished to its lunar reach
Becomes a kind of parable of incandescence.
Take a scene in a nightclub in war-torn France:
The smoke, the silverware, the sequined dress,
The bubbles orbiting a long-stemmed glass—

Who would interrupt them with a voice?
And then there's what happens to a face.
I wonder if I could get some silver nitrate
To take what I have to say and give it back
With a little of that luminescent silence. . . .
Not that I'd show a close-up of my face
Or anything that might be used as evidence;
There's not a single thing I wouldn't leave out.
But in silent movies when the screen goes black

It still feels as if there's something there.
Maybe it's the pervading threat of fire.
That's why they don't use silver nitrate anymore,
It's so flammable—that, and the cost of silver—
But in this case, I'd want it to explode.
In fact, clumsy as it is, it's my metaphor.
I admire Bashō, but I just can't buy
That bit about the wild geese and the cloud.
Unless he meant to float the possibility

That, after a season or two, the geese return.
It might even be implicit in the Japanese,
Which names a graceful but predictable species
Famous for going back to the same location.
You get to invent a poem in translation;
Only what isn't said is accurate.
For my haiku about friends that part,
I'd need the Japanese for *silver nitrate*,
A catchall character for *luminous* and *burn*.

Sonnet

I'd write a simple poem, not overlong,
Its details inexplicit, atmospheric,
Its pain inaudible, subsumed by lyric,
Its rhyming effortless, its meter strong.
It wouldn't lose itself in right or wrong,
The merely obvious or esoteric,
Would appear neither too calm, nor hysteric,
But pure, ethereal—such perfect song
That I could leave its bitter core behind
For good this time. Failure and injury
Just another piece of outlived story
With a beginning, middle and an end.
Let's try it then. Let singing start.
Why listen to an incoherent heart?

Lean Sonnet

Rain this time of year
means snow
on the mountains,
which means,
when the clouds lift, so
immaculate a white
I'm newly privy
to the secrets of the pure
of heart—my glimpse of grace:
only such sweet, unheavy
burdens that a simple spell
of heat or light could dissipate—
or the wherewithal
to spare the near white space.

Ghazal: Comet

Amidst our troubles, a sudden blessing:
Look up. There's a comet in the evening sky.

An omen for a pharaoh, caught retracing
Its half-forgotten summit in the evening sky;

Two burning tails—one gas, one ice—arousing
Ancient tumult in the evening sky;

Debris of a lost planet decomposing,
Gypsy diplomat in the evening sky;

Debut of life on earth, its ice dispersing
Facts too intimate for the evening sky. . . .

Traces of comet in us. This burning, this freezing?
Let's just blame it on the evening sky,

The music of the spheres in us, rehearsing
Across the gamut of the evening sky.

But—see?—the comet's already devising
A shortcut past the limit in the evening sky,

And when it comes again, we won't be witnessing.
Who will even claim it in the evening sky?

What's left of us may well be improvising
Our own last-minute plummet in the evening sky.

Analfabeta

For Laura Dondoli, in memory of her great-grandfather

I have a friend whose great-grandfather learned to read
From an uncle blinded in battle under Garibaldi;
He wanted Dante read to him aloud

And the boy learned to distinguish our unwieldy
Signs as simple sketches from his world,
Each with an unalterable melody:

Did he see two mountains touching, side by side?
They initiated *Magic, Music, Mastery.*
A three-pronged pitchfork's unsupported head?

Excellence, Echo, Elasticity.
A half-moon? Delusion. A full moon? *O.* . . .
And the boy, who was bright, apparently, as well as feisty,

Found out what he hadn't known there was to know:
That his own close-fisted, monotonous world
Would yield unmingled treasure, canto by canto—

That the unacknowledged mist inside his head
Could be converted to explicit rapture.
His uncle's illogical and graceless code

Would root out pervasive music anywhere,
A face one encounters always, once acquainted. . . .
But am I wrong in also thinking he learned more

Than those of us for whom someone merely pointed,
Uttering a too-fast string of monosyllables
(With one bright lingering W)? He circumvented

Our sullen lines and curves, random intangibles,
The shortest, quickest distances to sounds.
To him, markings on the page were parables:

Suns and stars were things a snake surrounds;
Vision started when a bird tried out its wings;
All imprinted words were loopy compounds

Of language's intent and actual things. . . .
I envy him. For me, it's artifice,
But every time he read, his uncle's moorings—

Does it look like the rind of a devoured slice
Of melon turned upon its side? That's C—
Kept him dreamily in place. . . .

Unless those early portraits fell away
And he, like the rest of us, just followed signs
Into the inner sanctum of what Dante—

Oblivious to his letters' prongs and wings and moons—
Required, simply, three strong rhymes to say.
My friend's grandmother remembered hearing lines—

Her father's favorites—almost every day.
He would read them, overcome, in the kitchen,
After which her mother would shrug and say

That the ravings of a drunkard or a madman
Would make more sense to her than all this poetry. . . .
Still, he'd read out line after line

And what I want to know is, did every Z
Flash—as he read along—with sudden lightning?
Was there an awkward kiss in every A?

Was each *H* a ladder with one rung?
And did he see on that one rung—like the runaway
Who stole his only brother's only blessing—

A sudden envoy, winged and otherworldly?
If so, was it climbing or descending?
Did it disappear or did it stay?

New Tanager/New Song

Sing God a new song, because He's done wondrous things.
                                        Psalm 98:1

A storm last night worthy of Sinai—
And the only sign of revelation:
A yellow-bodied bird in our undaunted tree,
Its crimson head and black-and-white striped wing
The flagrant markings of a western tanager,
Native to these parts, according to Peterson,
But not a specimen I've ever seen
In all my hours at this window, ogling.
I say it's an emissary from somewhere—

The dove and rainbow joined after the flood,
Or maybe a visitation from the outsized pages
Of the prized *Giant Golden Book of Birds*
I pored over incessantly in my childhood,
Learning to spot herons, egrets, mallards,
Orioles, auks, mergansers, partridges. . . .
My parents dreamed a future in biology;
They didn't know the danger signs of poetry:
The heady admixture of wings and words—

At that time, though, it was mostly wings—
That the real world contained such far-fetched things. . . .
To me, a city kid, it was a matter of faith;
All these species were purely theoretical,
Except for the occasional hygienic cardinal
Stopping for a dip in our neighbors' birdbath,
They weren't sights I ever thought I'd see—
But I believed in them, as I believed a sea
Had opened, years before that, for my family,

29

That a bush, in flames, might not burn away.
I loved the idea that, any time at all,
Some red or blue or gold might fly your way . . .
And limited my wish list to what was possible
In my relatively unambitious region:
The red-headed woodpecker, the orange oriole,
The goldfinch, and, especially, the scarlet tanager,
A choice piece of the Atlantic sky's bright theater:
Red from head to tail, its wings black satin —

At least that's how it looked in the illustration —
And after all these years, its western cousin
Has finally come to reward that little dreamer,
Whom I call up with the help of *my* eldest charmer,
A book open above her fallow homework,
Her heart set on some nonexistent page —
Maybe it will come to *her* in middle age? —
Or the baby, bringing me her dinosaur book
And repeating all the names with such concentration.

Actually, it's my middle one who most likes birds.
Penguins are her area of expertise
But — given the great distance to the Antarctic —
She's willing to help me scan local backyards.
In fact, on the tanager, she's my witness,
Not that she exactly shared my ecstasy
When we looked up the flashy bird's identity,
But the child's seven years old — how could she guess
What it's like to learn that, after all, a cherished book

Can coax the elements to keep its promise?
Who knew the universe was this magnanimous?
Don't worry—I can tell my girls—desires come!
All those earthly pessimists are wrong!
I really must try to sing a new song.
This is a world of wondrous things!
Who knows? I might even manage that poem
I've tried and failed to get at for so long
About the great blue heron stretching out its wings

Inches from our windshield on the Jersey turnpike.
We were in those overshadowed marshes,
So incongruous, really, opposite Manhattan's
Cocky, exhibitionist mirage—
Racing beside what I told the kids were bulrushes
(The very thing for prophets' camouflage!)—
And there it was: an arc of speed and plumage
Releasing its arrow—a majestic neck—
And, from nowhere at all, a blue expanse

Of wings. Not necessarily a miracle.
Marsh birds live in marshes, after all,
But—how can I explain it?— the Jersey turnpike,
Oil refinery, Newark airport, loading dock,
The earth—let's face it—as usual, a little wanting,
And here was this exquisite rising thing,
As if gravity had been a huge miscalculation.
Anything, when you think of it, could make an apple fall,
But what else could cause such exaltation?

Imagine life when such a sight was common,
Imagine all those herons left unseen. . . .
One era's commonplace is another's sign.
I wonder if it ever occurred to Einstein
That his theory of relativity applies to miracle;
He did have a certain reverence for the divine,
At least according to a famous story:
When asked what he'd have done if the empirical
Evidence had gone against his theory,

I would have taken pity on the Lord God,
He answered, *because the theory is correct.*
Which—if it questions God's inductive skills—
Does give Him credit for creation.
And God never aimed to be a theoretician;
He created first, then saw if things were good.
Still, maybe if He'd done some calculation
We'd have ended up with fewer troubles;
The ozone layer, for instance, might be intact,

The rain forests a little more resilient,
Every slip of sky ablaze with birds.
Still, it's no mean trick: a string of words
And light, darkness, water, dry land, sky. . . .
You can't really blame Him if, ebullient,
He was a little sloppy with some ingredients
Left lying around without even commandments
Not to go near them lest we die;
He thought he'd covered it with *Be fruitful and multiply,*

And even gave the birds a special blessing
Which worked in part; the adaptable ones are flourishing—
Falcons using skyscrapers as cliffs,
Eagles and seagulls gorging themselves at trash dumps—
No need to waste their time hunting and fishing;
Why shouldn't gulls and raptors have their Burger King?
Humans aren't the only ones progressing.
Next, maybe herons will renounce the swamps
For flooded basements; everyone makes tradeoffs. . . .

And who's to say it would be a bad thing?
My guess is the birds know what they're doing.
They've turned out to be evolution's geniuses.
I don't care if it's true. What a story!
Who says beasts aren't princes in disguise?
Millions of monsters, footloose in the skies!
Look it up! It's the latest theory:
Creatures so ungainly they could barely move,
Who were so—what?—determined? desperate? naive?

They trained themselves to hollow out their skeletons
And willed each clumsy scale into a feather.
This isn't poetic fancy. This is science.
Transfiguration! Beauty! Wondrous things!
My tanager's great-great-great-great grandfather
Was a dinosaur, who's not extinct, but sings,
And all these bird notes in the air are bulletins:
There is such an item as deliverance.
In a couple of eons, we, too, might sprout wings.

Yom Kippur Sonnet, with a
Line from Lamentations

Can a person atone for pure bewilderment?
For hyperbole? for being wrong
In a thousand categorical opinions?
For never opening her mouth, except too soon?
For ignoring, all week long, the waning moon
Retreating from its haunt above the local canyons,
Signaling her season to repent,
Then deflecting her repentance with a song?
Because the rest is just too difficult to face—
What we are—I mean—in all its meagerness—
The way we stint on any modicum of kindness—
What we allow ourselves—what we don't learn—
How each lapsed, unchanging year resigns us—
Return us, Lord, to you, and we'll return.

Villanelle from a Sentence in a Poet's Brief Biography

In '42 he was conscripted to work on trains.
An odd thing to mention in a poet's biography.
In '42? In Czechoslovakia? Trains?

I'm trying to figure out what this entry means,
If he sees himself as victimized or guilty.
In '42 he was conscripted to work on trains.

When Dutch workers wouldn't work *their* trains,
They found out that *work makes you free.*
In '42, in Czechoslovakia, trains

Weren't that busy. They didn't start the deportations
In earnest until 1943.
In '42 he was conscripted to work on trains.

But the next line says *after the war,* which means
That he was still at it in '43,
'44, '45. . . . In Czechoslovakia, trains

(What did he do? Run switches? Check the lines?)
Were as instrumental, let's face it, as Zyklon B.
In '42 he was conscripted to work on trains.
In '42. In Czechoslovakia. Trains.

Site of the Jewish Cemetery, Raciaz, Poland

Why care that there's a forest here
Where the cemetery used to be?
Fir trees, birch trees, pine trees, lovely markers.
And the local farmer's daughter
Who walks often in these woods
Can show you where the markers used to be;
She'll point out remnants of the layers of cement,
Which (according to my father-in-law)
Were made to look like bedclothes on the graves:
A few small clumps beneath the spreading trees,
Spreading out their roots among the bones,
Who might even enjoy the lively company.
And as for the markers, the stolen markers,
My guess is the bones don't miss them.
They know—don't they?—who they are.

A Footnote for Perets Markish

1895, Polonnaye, Ukraine–1952, Lubyanka Prison

There it was, Perets, your name
In an entry in Akhmatova's diary.
What you'd done was visit Nadezhda Mandelstam

Just after the local powers that be
Came for her husband (they'd get you later);
The only man to visit, according to the entry,

And nothing else about you. It doesn't matter;
To think Mandelstam might have been your friend,
As if poets come together before they scatter,

Like bits of paper clustered in the wind,
To wherever it is you go. Where are you, Perets?
I've tried and you're pretty hard to find.

Still, I doubt you'd have any regrets.
You must have been stubborn, an ideologue
Like you; I wish I could know I'd have your guts

Even if you're not in my on-line catalog.
But I also wish you could answer just one question,
Quickly, like Hillel, on one leg:

Which of your causes was crazier? The Revolution
Or spilling out your heart in Yiddish poems?
You could have saved a little something for Russian,

Or Hebrew even — don't lie — you knew its charms;
Communist or not, you once spent time in shul,
Extorting nimble secrets from the psalms

And then, one evening: an exquisite table
Set before you on the grass, and on your tongue
An intoxicating excess of the holy oil

Dripping from your forehead: you had to sing
And could hardly claim an instant so miraculous
In anybody else's mother tongue. . . .

Would you believe me, Perets, if I said I'm jealous?
It's my mother tongue — or should be — too
And the only one that might offer any solace

For how this vicious century has treated you,
As if there were any solace to be had. . . .
But the point is, Perets, I can't read you

Without the English on the other side
And — though I'm grateful for it — just between us
The translation isn't even all that good.

How could anyone sing in all this foreignness?
Though the bit about your *mother sewing* you *a shirt
Of the sky's bright linen* is a success

Even in English; its enormous heart,
So readily double-crossed by hopefulness,
Pulls mine — more cautious, paltrier — apart.

Or lines like: *I don't want to know what time it is,
I don't want to know my age —*
I could go on, there are enough of these

Favorite bits to fill page after page:
Make way, droplets of the sea, for one more drop—
But, clearly, if I really cared to salvage

The obstinate music the world let slip,
Like you, between the droplets of its sea,
I'd learn Yiddish till I could eavesdrop

On every single thing you had to say.
At the Workman's Circle, they have one volume;
Someone actually purchased one today—

Go after him—I told the guy—what's his name?
Did he use a check? A credit card? Is he still there?
Can I write him a letter? Will he translate them?

But the guy—quite a nice one, for an eight-hundred number—
Said the man bought lots of Yiddish poetry
And left. Was he old or young? He didn't remember.

You'll have to rely on him, Perets, not me.
I'm too lazy. I just want to talk to you
And could never get this language to convey

What yours manages to give off just by virtue
Of squeezing into an ill-suited script
Obsolescent two thousand years ago,

Though our stubborn ancestors continued to adapt
Its rococo crowns and stems to any sound
(This began, I guess, with orders barked in Egypt,

Ending—rather abruptly—in modern Poland).
Why waste time on some faddish alphabet?
It was hardly likely to be around

Beyond its civilization's puny orbit.
They meant the things they had to say to last,
And used the eternal *alef-bet*

Of a God they thought, if nothing else, was steadfast. . . .
You knew better, but you used it anyway,
Or maybe you weren't sure. It was a test

That He failed pretty spectacularly. . . .
Though who knows? Maybe I'm showing a lack of faith.
After all, someone bought your book today

And it's not even half a century since your death.
Maybe there will be a great revival;
Maybe the world's not ready for such wild breadth.

Think of Emily Dickinson and Melville.
Or perhaps you didn't know them? Think of Mandelstam.
Surely you never doubted his survival

Beyond his absurdly short, unpleasant lifetime.
But I came here to talk about you, Perets,
There are plenty of people talking about him.

I want to know what happened before those shots
In August '52, in the Lubyanka Prison.
You and the other poets, did you kibitz

For one last time, in the *mama-loshn*,
Pretending not to hear the order to fire?
There's a story about Emil Jannings, in Berlin,

Running out into the street with his Oscar
When the American army overran the place.
Don't shoot, he's said to have pleaded, *I win Oscar.*

You could have done that with your Lenin Prize,
Awarded—my anthology says—in '39,
But by then you must've known such things were pointless.

What wasn't pointless in the face of Stalin?
If only he'd forgotten you for one more year.
His successor was a good deal more humane,

A round feisty little man whom I remember
Banging shoes against a desk and saying *Nyet*.
It made an impression on me; I was four.

That's right, Perets, we might have met
If you'd stayed—when you had your chance—in the West.
You were even in Palestine, there's a poem about it;

But you went back to Russia, an idealist.
My bubbe's brother was like you; he stayed behind
When she went off to be a capitalist.

He didn't want to miss the promised land. . . .
Where is Polonnaye anyway? Maybe you knew him?
Isaac Medvedev? The friend, maybe, of a friend?

I know—many Yiddish speakers went in for communism—
But he was the one whose sister put him in an oven
To hide him when the Russian army came.

She used to laugh about that story, interwoven
Though it was with harrowing tidbits.
She forgot him till she went to light the oven;

She'd been so shaken by the bayonets,
The enormous officers—imposing, gruff—
Bellowing their vulgar language. You, Perets,

Must not have had a sister or an oven big enough,
Since it says you were a soldier in World War I.
So was my zayde, Yakov Osherov.

Maybe it was he you knew. A tailor? Thin?
I didn't know him either. Just like you,
He died before I managed to be born. . . .

But I've gotten off track—I usually do—
This wasn't supposed to be about my grandparents,
Though my bubbe was born the same year as you,

Or thereabouts. My father says, *What's the difference?*
Whenever I ask questions about these things.
He himself was among those infant immigrants

Forever to be jealous of their Yankee siblings,
Whereas I—perversely, I suppose—am a little vain
About his precarious beginnings

Where Russia and Belarus meet the Ukraine—
None of which has anything to do with you,
Except that your poems are, by rights, mine,

My legacy, my treasure . . . and I can do
Very little in the way of reading them;
It's only because of that diary I'm even writing you—

Only because you visited Nadezhda Mandelstam. . . .
Oh, but I was happy to see you there.
I remembered that *sky's bright linen* poem

And turned to the footnotes in the back with real pleasure,
Wondering what the editors would choose to say:
The Lenin Prize, of course; and maybe the editor

Would quote a stanza or two of yours, the way
He quoted the Russian poets who were mentioned.
Let me tell you, Perets, that usually,

When I'm reading a book, though I'm well-intentioned
About taking in each word, I'm a little slack
Even with footnotes helpfully positioned

At the bottom of the page, much less the back.
But *Perets Markish!* When I saw your name,
I turned to those notes like some monomaniac—

It wasn't just the thought that you knew Mandelstam
But, also, Perets, that he knew you,
Which meant maybe he regretted that not one poem

Of his ever suggested that a Jew
Had written it. . . . Who knows, maybe he,
Himself, could feel their Russian as askew,

The lush, borrowed, Jew-hating vocabulary—
Ice, bee, railway station, star—
As a traitorous offense to you, to me,

To the kindly, incomprehensible grandmother
He describes in a piece called *Judaic Chaos.*
He does state (I looked it up) very clearly there

That his father's was the Russian of the studious,
His mother's of the shaky first generation—
That he was the first of them to be at ease

With the greatness of the language, its tradition.
He never heard Yiddish till he was grown
But praises its perpetual interrogation,

Its *always surprised, always disappointed* tone,
Its *sharp accents always on the weakest syllables* . . .
A synagogue he calls a *Jewish ship*—in what ocean?

Steered by what? Prayer books? Bibles?
Poor Mandelstam, he didn't know who he was.
His father had abandoned all our valuables,

Chose Schiller, at fourteen, above rabbinic studies,
As you, Perets, unless I've pegged you wrong,
Chose Marx above yours—except the songs of praise,

Which had you since the *Hoshana Rabba* morning
When your father let you help him shake the palms
And the rivers clapped their hands, the mountains sang.

I also used to listen to those psalms
And know, though I couldn't make out a word,
That I was stumbling into dazzled realms;

I'm still wondering whom I overheard.
There *was* grandiose English to go along
But the way I remember it, its meaning blurred

Into the lavish, enigmatic string
Of gutturals, double vowels, double consonants;
I'd never known that syllables could sing. . . .

Don't misunderstand me, their magnificence
Was far more clear to me when I learned Hebrew.
Besides, that other, vaguer resonance

Is only audible when you don't need to know
The allotted limitations of each sound.
I wouldn't hear it, listening to you;

Besides, there isn't anyone around
Whom I could trust to read your poems aloud;
So I've been trying to stumble through *The Mound*

And can tell that *Hey, boundaries of the earth, spread*
Is *Hey, spread yourselves, boundaries of the earth.*
Either way, it's pure King David—

Either way, to me, it's surely worth
A thousand more familiar exhortations
In languages foisted on the earth

By a foolproof mix of currency and weapons—
At least of Yiddish this could never be said.
The earth couldn't even read your lines;

That's why its boundaries didn't spread.
But did I tell you? I spoke Yiddish at the Acropolis—
I met an Israeli whose grandmother had insisted

That he learn Yiddish; Hebrew wouldn't suffice;
She thought his chances in life would be imperiled,
Since Hebrew you could only use in one small place,

But you could speak Yiddish all around the world.
We laughed about it till we were in tears,
Wondering if the ancient pillars were startled

To hear a new language after all those years. . . .
Though I realize, now, they must have heard it from you
Or a few of the dreamers on those east-bound freighters

Who hadn't yet bothered to learn Hebrew.
You must have stopped en route to Jerusalem
To see what a little paganism could do. . . .

But I'm stalling, Perets, such a long poem
And there's something I haven't managed to say;
I did come fairly close another time,

But, to tell the truth, it isn't very easy.
It's that footnote, Perets, the one I told you about.
Remember? To that entry in the diary?

How I turned back excitedly to read it,
To see what they would put beside your name,
Wondering which poem they would quote?

Well, Perets, it listed all the women who came:
An actress, a critic, a poet's wife
(Gerstein, Olshevskaya, Narbut, you knew them?)

But nothing about you—almost as if
You were so ubiquitous, so famous,
That anything they could write about your life,

Your poetry, your death, would be superfluous. . . .
So I've said it. The editor left you out;
His field, I suppose, is Russian, not Judaic chaos,

But Judaic Modigliani got a footnote—
He and Akhmatova had a lovely, brief
Friendship in Paris. He sketched her portrait:

His ideal model—willowy, aloof—
She quotes him telling her, out of the blue,
J'ai oublié de vous dire que je suis juif.

I forgot to tell you I'm a Jew.
That's one thing, Perets, you never forgot—
You couldn't; it was written all over you—

And Mandelstam as well, at least that's what
It looks like to me from his photograph.
Tell me, Perets, did you ever meet?

Akhmatova's diary isn't exactly proof
And it's probably the only thing we've got.
She simply says you visited his wife;

Maybe it was a solitary visit—
Maybe you'd never seen the woman before—
You had connections, wanted to help a poet—

Or maybe you cherished her husband's friendship more
Than any link to anyone alive.
The piles of his letters in your drawer

Were enough to constitute a major archive;
Of course you burned them after his arrest,
As his wife burned yours . . . unless they survive

In a file somewhere . . . the army got them first. . . .
Ridiculous, isn't it, this speculation?
As you well know, what's lost is lost.

As if you could give a damn about your reputation.
But I'm sending that editor a biographical sketch
So he can change that footnote in the next edition,

Because I know a poem won't do much
And—even with such company as Fefer and Hofstein—
It's bad enough you're lying in that ditch

Without being utterly forgotten.
Or maybe you don't want to stay another minute
Even in the memory of a world this rotten. . . .

Maybe I should forget about my footnote—
Make that editor thoroughly erase your name—
Say Akhmatova was raving when she wrote—

Say that, in fact, that day, you never came,
You were too busy fighting for the Revolution
And, besides, despised that traitor, Osip Mandelstam—

Or maybe I'll send an anonymous quotation.
Oh, Perets, let me tell him it was you.
If I just quote the things you said to Samson—

The part that goes *Blind Samson, blind hero,*
Again hair is sprouting on your head—
Perets, would it be okay with you?

Or what if we forget that editor, forget you're dead?
What if we pretend I'm writing you?
What if hair *is* sprouting on your dreaming head,
Lost Perets Markish, lost hero?

III

Scattered Psalms

I (HANDIWORK/GLORY)

To the Conductor: A song of David.
The heavens declare the glory of God,
the firmament tells His handiwork.
Day on day utters speech,
night on night announces knowledge.
There is no speech and there are no words
without hearing their voice.

(Psalm 19:1–4)

Dare I begin: a song of Jacqueline?
But what, from my heart of hearts, do I say?
Not that it matters, since every line
Will murmur with the heavens, sotto voce,
The knowledgeable night, the chatty day,
Their information constant, simultaneous:
The glory of God and then *His handiwork.*
Indulge them: theirs is undiluted lyric
And we can't utter speech without its voice. . . .

So how hard could it be to write a psalm?
Think of David's fairly modest territory,
There are other trees than cedar, willow, palm
(*The handiwork of God* and then *His glory*),
So many kinds of praise he couldn't know:
The ferns on their unfinished violins,
The jonquils on their giddy, frail trombones,
The aspens shaking silver tambourines,
Then yellow-gold ones, then letting go.

What did David know about such changes?
The top arc of the spectrum gone berserk?
That when some skyward barricade unhinges
Without even a breath, a noise, a spark
(*The glory of God* and then *His handiwork*),
No single earthly thing stays as it was,
Except insofar as it still sings.
Hand me an instrument of ten strings;
Everything was put on earth to praise.

The crocodile. The cheetah. Hallelujah.
The nightingale. The lynx. The albatross.
The pine tree. Fir tree. Glacier. Hallelujah.
The hornet's diligence. The gibbon's voice.
The pale reprieve of snow. Hallelujah.
The volcano's unrestricted exultation.
The forest's lazy ease. The desert's fury.
Our own extraneous efforts at creation.
(*The handiwork of God* and then *His glory*.)

II (PURE SILVER/SEVEN TIMES)

The words of the Lord are pure words, refined silver
(clear to the earth)/ (in a furnace or the earth), purified
seven times.

Psalm 12:7

The degraded man says in his heart there is no God.

Psalm 14:1

Let's pretend, for an instant, we're not degraded,
That we'd know, if we heard it, the sound of pure silver
Fired in a furnace seven times.
Could it possibly be transcribed?
And if it's *clear to the earth*, who needs transcription?
And if it's *furnace of the earth*, why are we listening?
An earthly furnace for the words of God?

Unless David means his own earthly body,
How he crossed words out, rewrote them, seven times,
Or tried chanting them, his mouth not his,
Mumbling beneath his breath, there is no God
Unless He's here beside me, writing psalms,
Offering a kingdom for some molten words
Perfected in an oven seven times. . . .

Only David didn't say that about God;
That's an innovation of my own,
Which is why God never trusts me with His store of silver.
Imagine. All that untranslated vision,
The earthly furnace a courtesy to us,
To let us know how very lost we are.
God's refinements always come in sevens:

53

Here, too, the first brought light and, therefore, darkness,
The second worked to disentangle chaos,
The third divided fluid—meaning—from solid,
The fourth made a hierarchy of brilliancies,
The fifth made portions float while others soared,
The sixth refashioned it as human speech,
And the seventh gave it poetry, its Sabbath.

Unless it wasn't all that complicated:
God spoke to David from His holy mountain
And David was reminded of, say, Bathsheba's bracelets
As she took them off to come to bed.
It could be a matter of wishful thinking—
My friend who swears she saw her daughter, in a coma,
Move, when she asked her to, her arm.

But who's to say she didn't move her arm?
That when David lured Him with his purest words
God didn't answer from a holy mountain?
And even if *pure words* are an invention of desire
In the face of everything that's horrible
(Is that the earthly furnace seven times?),
Surely they are, nonetheless, still pure. . . .

Perhaps *clear to the earth* means transparent,
And all the words are written on the air,
A hundred thousand verses in the open space
Between me and these pages of the Psalms,
Each revised entirely by any passing breeze
As clouds and moon and stars plunder their silver
And sift it through the heavens seven times.

III (THRONES AND PSALMS)

God sat enthroned on the Flood.

Psalm 29:10

You are holy, enthroned upon the psalms of Israel.

Psalm 22:4

This is the way I like to think of Him:
Not on Ezekiel's throne of sapphires,
Which was only, after all, a likeness,
But held aloft by the religious ladies
(To whom I still owe eighteen dollars)
Who, every day, recite every psalm.
It's how they heal the sick (they saved my niece;
Her own doctors said it was miraculous),
Though surely it can't be just as afterthought
That they set up the place where God will sit. . . .

And what would it look like, this throne of psalms?
All those hallelujahs must be pillows—
Each one filled with cures for every malady
And hand-embroidered with a joyful noise—
The massive frame, the echo of God's own voice
Shattering Lebanon's unlucky cedars.
For decoration, there would be the letters:
The exotic *shin* with crowns, the ornate *tzadi*,
Arranged as leaping mountains, harps on willows,
Floods clapping their hands, upright palms. . . .

Unless it *is* those floods that are His throne.
I was never wild about that line,
But you can't really argue with destruction
And anyone can argue with a psalm.
A flood will diminish, on the other hand.
And who's to say what happens to a psalm?
If Noah had written one before the Flood
(Instead of getting so involved with gopher wood)
God might even have changed His mind
Or the music might have served as a distraction,

Which means, it seems to me, we'd better start singing
Or I'd better send those ladies my donation.
You know, the other day, that massive hurricane?
God just needed somewhere to sit down.
Or maybe—who knows?—He started thinking
And tears began to fall. It's not unusual.
He didn't even notice as they fell
And then—He had no choice—He blew His nose.
He never meant the dying and destruction.
All He wanted was a little praise.

IV (DARKNESS/WINGS)

*He mounted a cherub and flew, He swooped on the wings of the
wind. He made darkness His concealment, round Him His shelter—
the darkness of water, the clouds of heaven.*

Psalm 18:11–12

You will light my lamp, illuminate my darkness.

Psalm 18:29

I'll tell my daughter
Don't be afraid
It's only God
Hiding Himself
No need to worry yourself
About the dark
Imagine He's a rider
In a thick black cloth
What would lurk
In such a path?

And if she asks why God
Needs a hiding place?
Whom He's hiding from?
Who would know His face?
Do I tell the truth
Or keep it simple?
I could quote the psalm
For example
Fiery wrath
Wings outspread

But why the wings?
Why the cherub?
Why does God
Need a ride?
And what's it like
Mounting a cherub?
Does he buck
And flail his wings
Or nod
And glide?

And where
Will He alight?
Does He go far?
Maybe at the center
Of a dark ex-star
Whose energy?
Gravity?
Is so compact
It's far too strict
To let out light

A lamp unto my feet
Concealed in darkness
A light
To illuminate
The dark
A whirl of black
Its mass
So dense
That it was once
Pure light

Maybe each black hole
Is God concealed?
What do I tell
My daughter?
If the light's let out
What exactly is revealed?
Darkness of water
Darkness of cloud
Don't be afraid
It's only God

V (PSALM 37 AT AUSCHWITZ)

Nourish yourself with faith.

Psalm 37:3

*Just a little longer and there will be no wicked one; you'll
contemplate his place and he'll be gone.*

Psalm 37:10

*I was young; I've also grown old, and I've never seen a righteous
man forsaken or his children begging bread.*

Psalm 37:25 and
Birkat Hamazon (Grace after meals)

All those boys who'd started heder at three,
After licking a page of letters smeared with honey,
Who, legend has it, by the age of ten,
Could track the route of an imaginary pin

Stuck through the Gemara, word for word—
Surely it was nothing to the likes of them,
Who clung to every holy thing they heard,
To learn by heart the words of every psalm,

And surely, even given the odds, one,
Despite his scholar's pallor and his puniness,
Made it, by some miracle, to the workers' line
And didn't go directly to the gas.

What I want to know is: could he have tried,
Before his slow death from starvation,
To bring himself a little consolation
By reciting all those psalms inside his head?

Just a little longer and there will be no wicked one
He'd murmur to a shovel full of ash,
You'll contemplate his place and he'll be gone.
Unless he was too busy saying kaddish

For his father—lost a few days before
Along with his own reservoir of psalms,
Still stunned by the crudeness of the cattle car,
A man known to go hungry giving alms,

Who'd walk to shul the long way, on a muddy road,
So as not to crush a blade of grass on Shabbos—
Was he to say his father wasn't righteous
That his only son should go in search of bread?

Though the psalm does say *begging* bread,
And begging was of little use at Auschwitz:
There, you had to have something to trade—
A sock, a shoe, a blanket, cigarettes—

For what someone who did favors for a dishwasher
Had managed to scrape off dirty SS plates.
Our scholar wouldn't eat—it wasn't kosher—
Though the rules didn't really apply at Auschwitz;

The Torah, after all, says, *to live by them,*
You can even eat vermin in the face of death;
But our young man kept singing that one psalm
Over and over: *Nourish yourself with faith*

(Is that why David says he's never seen
The children of the righteous begging bread?
They're meant to be sustained by faith alone?)
And was our scholar, singing that line, comforted?

And his fellow prisoners? Could they have heard?
Did he sing the other psalms or just that one?
Maybe all the psalms had left his head.
He'd contemplate their place and they'd be gone.

I could try asking my father-in-law
If, in all his years at Auschwitz-Birkenau,
He ever once overheard a psalm.
But I know the answer, just imagining him

Giving me the slightly baffled stare
He keeps in reserve for these conversations
That says: Where do you find these foolish questions?
And then: How could you know? you weren't there;

If I hadn't been, I wouldn't believe it either. . . .
Aloud, he'd tell me: *Psalms, I didn't hear,*
You were lucky to put two words together
Without some SS screaming in your ear,

But this was nothing. This was nothing.
Most of his descriptions end like this.
He almost never says what *something* was.
Whatever it may have been, he'll always sing

That bit about the children begging bread
When it's quoted in the *Birkat Hamazon.*
I refused to sing it as a kid—
Though, unless you're counting television,

I could honestly have said I'd never seen,
Or known I'd seen, a single person starving—
My poor rabbi found me so unnerving
When I'd balk at his effort to explain

That the line wasn't meant to be historical
But something to hold onto as a dream.
I love to sing it now—only a fool
Would try to be literal about a psalm—

But then I'd argue: *but it says seen.*
The past tense. A single person's life span.
Read it. *I've been young and I've grown old.*
Even now, singing it, I'm still compelled

To wonder what the line's supposed to mean.
Maybe the key word really is *seen*
And David's trying to make us a confession:
That, for all his affect of compassion,

He never, even once, bothered to look.
Or maybe it was just that he couldn't see.
A man who, as a child, with a sling and rock,
Could conquer a nation's greatest enemy. . . .

A slingshot at Auschwitz? Can you imagine?
Though once, in a film, I heard a Vilna partisan
Describe his girlfriend crippling a Nazi train
Loaded with guns and bombs and ammunition

With a single handmade ball of yarn and nails. . . .
But that was only one Nazi train.
She did, for a week or so, tie up those rails,
But, before she knew it, trains were running again,

Taking whoever hadn't died of gunshots
In graves they'd dug themselves in nearby woods
To slower but less messy deaths at Auschwitz—
Some with entire books inside their heads—

And what I'm saying is, there were so many of them—
Let's forget about my scholar with the shovel—
I'll admit it; he had no thought of a psalm—
But think of the others, many religious people,

Standing there, waiting in the other line,
First, for the barber, to have their hair cut,
Then, for whoever did the tooth extraction,
All these things took time; they had to wait.

I know it sounds crazy, but couldn't one of them—
Not that it matters, they all died anyway—
But still, so many people, and enough time
For reciting what the dying are supposed to say

(*Hear, O Israel,* et cetera) *and* a psalm.
Or not even a whole psalm. Just one line.
All those people waiting. Couldn't one of them
Have mumbled to a brother, a father, a son

(The women, of course, were on another line
And this was not a psalm they would have known),
Just a little longer and there will be no wicked one;
Just a little longer . . . he'll be gone.

VI (SUDDEN *MICHTAM*)

To the Conductor, a plea to be spared from destruction, by David,
a michtam (Psalm 57:1)

> And suddenly what I'm reading is a *michtam.*
> I look at a number of English versions—
> Not knowing what a *michtam* is—and every
> Last one of them—some still collecting royalties—
> Tells me what I'm reading is a *michtam.*
> Oh, thank you, King James; thank you, Rabbi Hillel
> Danzigher; thank you, translation committee
> Of the Jewish Publication Society;
> But couldn't you do a little better than *michtam?*
>
> Luckily, the Hebrew-English dictionary
> (The Alcalay, a three-volume set)
> Through which I always travel very slowly,
> Says: *epigram, aphorism, golden poem.*
> And mentally I write a thank-you note
> To Mr. Alcalay: My dear R. Alcalay,
> If there is ever anything you need—
> A letter of recommendation, a poem,
> Advice on the niceties of English—
> Please don't hesitate to ask me.
> And another one to Rabbi Danzigher,
> With a duplicate to JPS:
> Though it's a bit expensive, I'd direct you
> To the Alcalay Hebrew-English Dictionary,
> Where it says that *michtam* is a golden poem,

65

The very phrase my bubbe would have used
If she'd made it to a hundred-one;
In her no-longer-thriving native tongue
There is no higher praise than *goldene*.
On the telephone, she would have told her friends,
Though she'd have understood barely a third of it:
You should see my Jackie's golden poem.

To my bubbe, I'd have written *michtam*
Upon *michtam*. Who decides when it's a *michtam?*
Maybe the person who wrote down the psalms
Was actually Obed, David's grandfather
(His grandmother wouldn't have learned to write
And, anyway, we're never told her name)—
So dazzled by the *apple of his eye*
Who sang his *alef-bet* at eighteen months,
The Song of the Sea, by heart, at three:
Conductor, hear my David's golden poem.

Was David thinking of him when he wrote
May you look upon your children's children?
You made it, bubbe, even if your boys
Were not quite *olive plants around your table,*
Though one was a hell of a basketball player,
And my father, the *goldene neshumeh,*
Would walk around the house reciting Shakespeare,
Though now he claims to need help with my poems—

He'd understand if I could write a *michtam,*
But I can't do better than a *michtav,*
Of which I've written more than a fair number.
Maybe, since a *michtav* is a letter,
A *michtam*'s an epistolary psalm.
It's not a bad idea, a letter to God:

You could collect your thoughts that way
Or, better yet, decide not to send it
As I decide with nearly all my letters,
Or sloppiness dictates, since I lose them all,
Or am incapable of having stamp,
Letter, envelope, correct address
All in the same place at the same time,

None of which is necessary for a poem.
But what is required of a *michtam?*
A living grandmother? a ten-string harp?
What's missing from the last three thousand years?

A Jesuit priest, in the Anchor edition,
Which I smuggled from the synagogue library,
Suggests that *michtam* means *inscribed in stone,*
And while I have nothing against Jesuits—
Indeed, I've always thought they think like Talmudists—
This is not the meaning of a *michtam.* . . .

The words of a *michtam* are pure gold
Inscribed with the feather of a turtledove
On parchment from the skins of newborn lambs
Immaculate enough to serve as sacrifices
As the sun goes down on *Hoshana Rabba*
(With ivory altars, knives of beaten gold)
And one more book of life is sealed for good.

Or perhaps they place their impress on the wax
That seals the book, or other vital messages,
Unless, of course, they're not inscribed at all
But clamor when the sunlight on still waters
Gathers in the willows' fleeting gold
Just before they weep themselves to sleep

Or rise out of the *lai, lai, lai*'s I substitute
For a lullaby's forgotten Yiddish lyric
Though most of the children from that noisy world
Who wouldn't go to bed without its golden tune
Have already fallen fast asleep.

VII (*MICHTAM*/DOVE/DISTANT SILENCE)

A *michtam*; on *JONATH ELEM REHOKIM* (loosely, *the dove
of the silence of the distance*)   Psalm 56:1

*My wanderings You Yourself have numbered, place my tears
in Your flask, are they not in Your book?*
                                                    Psalm 56:9

> Our great Rashi says the dove is David
> (Defenseless before his Philistine captors,
> The note continues, like a silent dove).
> Another rabbi says a musical instrument,
> And the King James, ever graceful, just gives up:
> *To the chief musician upon JONATH ELEM REHOKIM.*
> The JPS's rabbis do the same thing
> But add my favorite scholarly note:
> *Meaning of the Hebrew uncertain*—
> A sentence calling out for poetry.
> Who will blame me if I get it wrong?
>
> I can't do as badly as the Artscroll edition,
> Which calls it *the distant dove of silence,*
> Or the wishful Jesuit of the Anchor version,
> On the lookout, I suppose, for the trinity
> (A dove in paintings means the Holy Ghost)
> Who calls it *the dove of silent Gods.*
>
> Take my word for it: it's a misreading
> And David must have known his Hebrew grammar—
> Unlike the rabbi of the Artscroll edition—
> There's no way that's a distant dove

The dove of silence beyond reach
The dove of silence inaccessible
The dove of the silence of distances
The dove of the muteness of the distance

Oh, but surely this is Noah's dove,
I'd know him anywhere, his baffled ear
Still a little startled by the soundlessness
Of a dazed world emerging from a flood.

No one would ever count his wanderings
Except for a single vocal olive branch,
And as for his tears, if a dove cries tears,
They fell into the not yet quiet sea. . . .

And if it is a musical instrument,
How would it sound, this dove of distant silence?
Do you blow against a reed or pluck its strings?

And another question: who wrote that bit
About wanderings numbered in a book?
Is someone here pretending to be David?
Samuel 1 and 2 weren't written yet,
Unless—who knows?—David wrote those too,
Afraid that no one else would get them right. . . .

Though his *I* could just be the Jewish *I*
Of the exhausted ex-slave in all his wanderings,
Since, in a brilliant propaganda coup,
We're obligated yearly to insist that *we*
(And not just our fathers' fathers' fathers)
Were brought out of Egypt by an outstretched hand

(I for one could swear that I remember it—
Or perhaps it's the ten commandments I remember—
I was very young and there was thundering
And then a soothing sound, like far-off doves).

Of course he must be talking about the Torah,
But what about this flask? this tear-filled flask?
What would God want with such a thing?
Unless it's the secret drinking source
Of the dove of an evanescent hush.

Maybe someone else *did* write this poem,
Some musical prodigy who knew how to play
The dove of inaccessible silence,
But first he had to string it with purple threads
Unraveled from a high priest's holy garments

And tune it to the bass note of the twisted horn
Found tangled in a thicket near a rock
Where a mosque would one day quarrel with a
        missing Temple,
And where, if He's anywhere, God hovers still,
Collecting samples for His flask of tears.

Unless the instrument's not stringed at all
But a complicated flute: mother-of-pearl
From a chambered nautilus that Jonah pulled
Out of the whale's belly as a souvenir.

It makes a high, transparent, cooing sound
But only with a reed devised of bulrushes
Salvaged out of Moses' makeshift ark
Or a braid of Absalom's unwieldy hair. . . .

The dove of a silence beyond reach
The dove of not quite certain sacred tongues
The dove of numberings, of wanderings
The dove of branches undeterred by floods
The dove who gathers tears in a heavenly flask

And uses them to cleanse a distant instrument
Which, when he holds it, sometimes sounds by accident,
Its unimaginably subtle notes
Diminishing with each new rank of cloud

Until even their soundlessness is lost to us
Except as rumors in sporadic drops,
A shade impure for their celestial task,
Falling back, unsure of what they've heard.

VIII (AT THE GALLERIA DELL'ACCADEMIA: PSALM 51)

Lord, open my lips, and my mouth will tell Your praise.
                                                    Psalm 51:15

Is that what he's saying? You can't be sure,
And this isn't the usual stance of prayer;
Still, it's what I hear as I look at him—
Not that he requires any psalm—
But here they all are, as yet unwritten:
The cedars whole, the mountains motionless,
The oceans' hands unruffled by applause
And stirring anxiously within the stone
Their soon-to-be-discovered hallelujahs. . . .

I say the slingshot is a metaphor,
That if there's any sign of a Goliath here
It's that once undifferentiated block of stone,
Which seemed to utter, from its holy mountain:
Cleanse me with hyssop and I shall be clean
(After Bathsheba, the psalm says, the ordeal with Nathan,
But this David is clearly thinking of Jonathan),
Wash me; I'll be whiter than snow.
And he is, except for a disintegrating toe

Left to stand too long in the open air—
Which, with the softness of his open face—
Makes him look peculiarly defenseless;
He doesn't really seem like any warrior
Though I used to think I saw ferocity
In his profile (his full face held the poetry);
Now I see it's all diffused by awe
And the still unsorted-out intensity
That hasn't yet come up with *hallelujah*

Or calculated what it takes to climb
The as-yet-uncharted mountain of the Lord;
Only Michelangelo has figured
That out. But when you look across the room
You see that his solution didn't last;
He grew impatient with his own perfection—
As if he switched allegiances to Samson,
Wanting not mere giants but a whole foundation,
Even if it meant that he, too, would be lost—

And gave up easy strength to try to excavate
Some dim volcanic memory in the stone.
Was it worth it? The David's more famous
But think of what it took to call away
A face like Matthew's from that unhewn stone—
Or for these prisoners to smuggle out
Even a hint of torso, shoulder, thigh. . . .
Each is a definitive self-portrait,
More accurate, surely, than the Nicodemus,

Who grieves above Christ dying down the street
With a pieced-together misproportioned arm.
Maybe it's just Christ's arm he's grieving for;
Michelangelo smashed it with a hammer
(He still required perfection; I was wrong)
But after his death, someone mended it
And, from many angles, it's sublime,
Though Michelangelo was right; the arm's too long.
Who knows? Perhaps he worried about the psalm:

Eyes they have, but they see not; ears they have. . . .
He'd meant that *Pietà* for his own grave
But who was he to give God's son an arm?
Or maybe, old now, he'd reread each psalm
And realized he'd even gotten David wrong—
This boy would never cry: *O Lord, how long?*
Or notice *the groaning of a prisoner*
Even across a room—gasping for air?
Or prying lips apart to mouth a prayer?

IX (LOOKING THROUGH THE WINDOW: PSALM 121)

I will lift my eyes to the mountains, where
my help will come; my help from God, who
makes heaven and earth.

Psalm 121:1–2

Was it Jonathan Edwards who'd repeat, continually,
One verse from the Song of Songs for an entire day?
I am the rose of sharon, the lily of the valley.

He believed that, in the repetition,
He could hear Christ's voice replace his own.
And while a god who'd use that kind of self-description

Would put me off—mine asks sarcastic questions
Like *Where were you when I laid earth's foundations?*—
I'm also given to wild expectations.

Here's my secret: help does come
When you invoke it with the hills or even hum
The melody for that one bit of psalm.

It's the sheer idea of lifting up your eyes,
The heady speculation that the mountains rise
Purely for the sake of lifting us,

As if the endless business of creation
Required even our participation.
But wouldn't we know it? It's a wild notion;

Besides, it's no mean trick to lift your eyes
And I've been making an untenable promise
In my impatience to repeat the phrase

That requires nothing of me: *help will come*—
It *is* an extraordinary claim—
I will lift my eyes to the mountains—pure momentum

Could make anything happen after that—
Unless it's part of a triumvirate:
Lifted eyes, my help, the mountains' height—

All approximations for the undiluted
And various emergences of God
A little like gas and liquid and solid

Versions of something wholly without substance.
But then—is it my failing?—there is a chance
That all I'll know of real deliverance

Is these blue-white mountains out my window
Still reeling from this morning's blast of snow.
They're uncannily beautiful without the Hebrew

So why don't I leave well enough alone?
Surely it's enough: a diamond-studded mountain.
Why insist on making it a stand-in

For what, if we could lift our eyes, we'd see.
(What help do I need? What is wrong with me?)
A lifted eye, a lily of the valley.

X (SNOW PSALM, TO THE CONDUCTOR,
ON *JONATH ELEM REHOKIM*)

For this, we'll need our doves again.
See how they have turned the sky their color,
Tempering the air's reluctant pallor
With a gray, iridescent discipline,

As if each cloud's escaping cargo
Had a fringe of doves on its circumference,
Wings arced at a respectful distance
From the unsuspected resonance of snow—

Music of hexagons? Music of whiteness?
Music of a heaven's hardened tears?
Music of the calm interstices
Between the shedding sky's abandoned layers,

The willows' fallow harps restrung with snow
And hills awakening their instruments
With variations on a rumored silence,
Its feathers' shallow plunge, its startled coo.

XI (DEAD MEN'S PRAISE)

Yakov Glatstein already
used this verse in a poem,
translated, in that book
(*Radiant Jews*, 1946),
Dead Men Don't Praise God

and you can see how, then,
it must have seemed that, for years,
this verse had festered in its psalm
waiting to reveal its acrid heart.

I don't blame him if he thought
all praise had ended

but I wonder if it's heartless
after only fifty years
to think—again—the praise has just begun:

The dead don't praise God,
or the ones who go down to silence,
but we'll praise God
from now on forever
hallelujah—

I'm not suggesting that we think about it:
just sing it, during Hallel,
at synagogue, the next new moon,

and get in on a little
of its stubborn bravado,
its delirious proof
of itself—*hallelujah*—

which, in my opinion,
explains the annoying epithet *chosen*
that has caused us so much trouble over the years

(though there are a host
of twentieth-century explanations:
chosen for suffering, for near-annihilation,

or—on the other hand—for the idea
of public ownership of means
of production, relativity,
A la Recherche du Temps Perdu).

I say: chosen for this
tenacious language,
to be the *we*
who get to say this word
and live forever,

and it makes me pity Handel,
gospel singers, televangelists—
belting out their hearts for a borrowed word—

when I have the whole thing,
one hundred and fifty psalms,
every single syllable a *hallelujah*

and not—you have to understand—
an English hallelujah
with its vague exultation and onomatopoeia

but a word composed of holy signs
that could actually spell God's name
if they weren't ordering the universe
to praise Him.

There's a story my friend Isaac tells
before he reads *Akdamut* on Shavuot:

how the poet Rabbi Meir ben Yitzhak
first wrote *Akdamut* in Hebrew
and the angels stole it away, page by page,

so he had to begin all over again,
this time in Aramaic,
to keep his genius secret from the angels.

I want to know how David
got away with it.

Were the angels just so riveted
by what they heard
that they left him to go on and on and on?

(With Glatstein, there wasn't any problem;
they were probably in stitches:

this poor *shlemazel* writing
in an instantaneously dead language —
irony's the soul of Yiddish —
dead men don't praise. . . .)

As for me, though it's my new goal
to have a page or two stolen by an angel

(it would have to be—let's be realistic—
a fairly boorish angel, not much of a reader,
the eyes on his wings pressed shut,

so addicted to watching television—
mostly telenovelas—he knows
the English language by osmosis).

I don't figure this page is in imminent danger.

Maybe, reading over his shoulder,
the angels rejected David's poem
(didn't they have enough of praising God?)

or maybe—that's it!—it was they who fed him lines
(*Do you think this kid will really take over? hallelujah!*)

or maybe it's nonsense about the *Akdamut* . . .
there was no Hebrew version,
are no angels . . .

and my *hallelujah,*
my precious, rising *hallelujah,*
doesn't have the stamina
I need it for,

has, in fact, been burned away
before it could adorn a single tongue
for countless generations of David's offspring

and I'm not talking about the ones who turned to ash—
they're around somewhere, singing *hallelujah*—

I'm talking about the other ones, numberless as stars,
who never got to sing a word at all:

permutations of permutations
of permutations of permutations
of pairs of double helixes,

singular and brief as snow,
among the double helixes that burned,

every one an unrepeatable
and complex promise,

and, among them,
certainly, at least
a few who might
have liked, even for
an instant, to live forever.

XII (SCIENCE PSALM)

The heavens are the heavens of God,
and the earth He gave to man.

Psalm 115:16

They will fear You as long as the sun and moon endure.

Psalm 72:5

Scientific evidence is nothing to rabbis—
Bring them some ancient rocks, carbon-dated,
And they'll say *so God created the world old . . .*
(I mean, of course, the ones who still insist
That fifty-seven-hundred years ago the Lord created
Everything in seven days, including rest),
And the rabbis have a point—though I'm not sold—
Since what are a couple of allosaurus vertebras

To a Guy whose single word produces light?
My Hebrew teacher told us about a Yemenite
Who, against the solemn oath of television,
Dismissed the moon landing as a fraud.
The heavens are the heavens of God,
And the earth He gave to man was his position—
He needed a different kind of imagination
Or, at least, a better definition.

Earth means whatever's given to us,
Which now includes the moon and, shortly, Mars.
I'm inclined to welcome the new expanse
Since, otherwise, this is all there is,
And I like picturing myself among the ancients,
This English of mine a language safely dead,
And schoolchildren uncertain whether Xerxes, El Cid,
Or Jimmy Carter fought the Trojan Wars,

Giggling, no doubt, at the ridiculous lengths of time
It took our crude machines to get to Saturn . . .
Relativity, if not utterly forsaken,
Evolved into a simple grade-school theorem.
(Amazing what such primitives could discern!)
Why should our particular errors last?
And what chance is there, given our record in the past,
That, in anything at all, we're not mistaken?

Is *accuracy* that heaven, only God's?
Don't laugh. It isn't utterly impossible;
Who's to say it doesn't exist somewhere,
A place, by definition, inaccessible,
But pleasant to believe in, nonetheless,
Since, if it existed, God would also be there,
And maybe even—though I'm not laying any odds—
They'll end up finding Jews in outer space,

In some backwater galaxy, studying Torah,
Not a single word diverging from ours;
They'd be up there, oblivious, thinking *theirs*
Is the heaven and earth Moses was talking about.
And why not? Maybe ours is a dry run,
It would explain that line about the moon and sun—
Why would God rely on such ephemera?
He *must* be banking on that other planet.

There could be a spare Jerusalem just sitting there—
No suicide bombs, no checkpoints, no soldiers—
Its Holy Temple still intact!
And we could do an airlift of the Lubavitchers;
We'll tell them Rabbi Schneerson will meet them there,
Most of his disciples are already packed.
(He's expected to rise from the dead
Any minute now—real estate has skyrocketed

Around the Queens cemetery where he's buried;
They all want to be first in his entourage.)
We'll send along sufficient stores of kosher meat
(They'd never trust the butchers on another planet)
And stones, in case some women try to pray. . . .
It beats coming to America in steerage,
Not quite as crowded, if a bit more hurried,
And, in terms of going home, no farther away. . . .

But where did this come from, wasn't I writing
A poem about how we can't know anything?
(Not, admittedly, the most original subject
But one, it seems to me, you have to face.)
Still, when there's no sign of an obliging muse,
If you've got to be wrong, you might as well be funny;
And even if a muse showed up now, I suspect
I wouldn't have the heart for the uncanny

Intimacy of what would have to follow—
That is, with any muse who pulled her weight.
I'm not entirely ready to disintegrate
In the face of the encyclopedic darkness
Which is—isn't it?—my subject here:
A nothingness so stringent and so thorough
That it conveys intelligence, however imprecise,
Of just how comprehensively you'll disappear.

Is it possible you don't know what I mean?
So familiar, so regular, it would be comforting
If it didn't bring such undiluted terror—
Which is where this religion stuff comes in;
It has an obsessive way of diverting
Your attention, and, though it's anybody's guess,
The rabbis have put three thousand years into this
And I don't much go in for trial and error.

Besides, imagine actually believing
That the old bearded rebbe to whom my grandma used to point
From her Parkway bench on Shabbos afternoon
(Not that I knew which guy in a black caftan
With a big black hat and long gray beard she meant)
Is going to rise from the dead and take me with him—
I, for one, am quite attached to living;
Don't think I wouldn't be tempted, if he came,

To sit in the women's section for all eternity,
A wig on my head, my knees and elbows covered. . . .
On second thought, some fates are worse than death.
Sorry. Enough jokes. I take that back.
I believe—despite my weakness for a wisecrack—
That something or other has to be revered,
And the truth is I envy those people's faith
Even if I do think they're all *meshugene*

And, worse, true enemies of peace;
But I'm not talking politics in all this darkness.
I'm just looking for a little light,
And please don't point me to those fly-by-night
Creations: the stars and moon and sun—
As far as I'm concerned, their deadline's passed.
God, was there nothing tougher you could give to man?
I'd so like something that will last.

XIII (SPACE PSALM)

Let stars reverse their courses—hallelujah—
Let planets flaunt their necklaces of ice—
Let suns confound eclipses—hallelujah—
Let moons' scavenged radiance rejoice—

Let galaxies recluster—hallelujah—
Let nebulae uncloud and celebrate—
Let meteors spread banners—hallelujah—
Let black holes unleash astonished light—

Let comets jump their orbits—hallelujah—
To jangle inadvertent atmospheres
With rumors of the distance—hallelujah—
Anecdotes—songs—suspicions—prayers

IV

One Last Terza Rima/ Italian Train

Why, always, this compulsion to explain?
Who cares that I can't bear to close my eyes
Despite some thirteen hours on a plane,

That, as far as I'm concerned, if there's a muse,
It's snatches of Italian conversation on a train
And just this aggregate of shrubs and trees:

Umbrella pine, olive, willow, whitethorn,
Even in this ratty bit of countryside
Between Fumicino and the Rome station. . . .

Sicknesses, headlines, daughters getting married
(I actually learned Italian on such a train;
I'd use Spanish and get corrected)

Join forces with the engine's constant motion
To smooth whatever I may have to tell
With a whimsical, but resolute, percussion—

The occasional blooming almond's a clanging cymbal;
The whitethorn's bramble, a sort of snare
(You can almost hear the *swish* as its branches reassemble

Whenever the racing window comes too near,
Solicitous, no doubt, about that stash of whiteness,
As yet undelivered, though the air

Has started making its yearly balmy promises).
And the umbrella pines, beneath their spreading roofs,
Make a noise between a whisper and a hiss

As if trying, discreetly, to get the olives'
Attention, while they, in turn, mimic the triangle
With an intermittent *ping* of silver leaves. . . .

This is a bit fanciful, but it's an angle;
I haven't even had coffee, much less sleep,
And the way the language and the train ride mingle

With the muted winter contours of this landscape
Just *is* the stuff of poetry to me.
Or maybe it's my own lucky apprenticeship

I'm talking about: it was in Italy
That I—rich, from leaving a tenement apartment
Near Bloomingdale's—started writing every day;

Too bad I never told Cohen Brothers' Development
(The name on my twelve-thousand-dollar check)
Precisely how their money was being spent;

They ought to have been able to get a tax break,
A Cohen Brothers' Fellowship in poetry,
And—unlike me—they had some lousy luck;

One lady on rent control wouldn't move away
So they had to build their skyscraper around her
(It's on sixtieth, near Lex, to this very day;

You can take the 4, 5, 6, N, or R;
I used to be a wiz on the New York subways,
But the stops I rarely used are now a blur,

Since I moved to a city that has no subways,
Just buses that call it quits at nine or ten
And hit only the ski resorts on Sundays).

I should track those Cohen brothers down;
Could have ended up in law school without them,
Had already handed in my application. . . .

But what would I do? Accuse or thank them?
No, that's disingenuous. I like this life
Of waking in the morning to check the poem

I worked on the day before for signs of life;
I like finding rhymes, turning a phrase,
But at the same time, I know I'm fooling myself:

It's not as if I don't know what a poem does—
You anointed my head with oil; my cup runneth over;
The top of your head comes off, as Emily says;

Some essential bit of life changes forever. . . .
Every cup you see—and that's only a translation—
Is suddenly impatient to deliver

An inexhaustible reserve of exaltation;
Don't tell my husband, but sometimes, when he's asleep,
Something inexplicable in his expression

Or his endearing murmuring (he does that in his sleep)
Makes me think my own cup's running over . . .
No need for another phrase . . . my cup. . . .

So, the question should be, what am I doing here,
Going to all this trouble with terza rima
When I can't come up with a line for my one lover?

It's a kind of self-delusion, terza rima—
As if all I need is one more rhyming word,
And I'll possess this changeless panorama,

This chanting train, these echoes in my head,
These effusive strangers making conversation
And force them into one sustaining chord

With Laura's ancient Renault at the station,
My first jolt of Lavazza at the bar,
The batmobile I bring Lorenzo, his jubilation. . . .

One more rhyme—then a new one—then one more
Like drops of whatever filled that waiting cup
Until mine, too, eventually runs over;

But this thing I'm pouring into won't fill up . . .
And even if it did, who would see?
I doubt that anyone would actually take a sip,

As I'm obliged to do at any gallery:
Derain, of all people—not even a favorite—
Pressed a little vista on me recently

That made me acknowledge, whether I wanted to or not,
How the bridge from Charing Cross (which I thought I knew
From several vantages, by train, on foot)

Isn't black at all, but electric blue,
The towers of parliament are shamrock green—
And pink and mauve are the London sky's true

Colors. No more gray! no more wrought iron!
Such an improvement on the dour place I knew—
My apologies, dear, underrated André Derain;

How have I ever lived without you?
And all that from one inadvertent look.
Too late, I realize I've chosen the wrong milieu:

No one has to go and order Derain's new book,
Open it, proceed, line after line,
Push beyond what's inexact or cryptic,

Realize his mind is wandering, begin again. . . .
Derain only needs a single well-placed wall,
And even a person paying poor attention

Will buy whatever it is he has to sell.
I ran around—I was in the National Gallery,
Playing hooky from the Vietnam Memorial

And the Holocaust Museum, which I'd planned to see—
Looking for some maneuver I might use
And there was the stunning painting of the girl in the red beret

(Beady eyes too close together, horsey nose);
How the hell did Vermeer manage that?
A useful trick, to be able to transpose

(She's in a nearby painting also, different hat)
Homely to lovely, since most things aren't beautiful—
I suppose that's why a person becomes a poet,

Though it's an elusive promise to fulfill—
Which explains, I suppose, what I'm doing here.
Not that Foligno Station is all that beautiful,

But Laura and I will get into her car
And soon we'll be moving through a gold medieval town
Whose triumvirate (trinity?), wall, cathedral, tower,

Has thus far never let it down.
And there will be no sign of expired ugliness,
Only the supreme amnesia of the stone. . . .

I'm beginning to think that's why we die—our memories
Are too precise; take my father-in-law
And the ugly things he knows;

How the world will prefer itself when what he saw
No longer deadens his or any eyes
(Or is it more like an abrasion of the cornea

Singeing every other thing he sees?),
When no blue numbers under summer sleeves
Take observant children by surprise.

After all, there aren't any graves
Except for the occasional unmarked forest,
And such places will again be pleasant enclaves

Like the picnic grounds and campsites in the vast
Tracts of seemingly untainted acres
Where I live, in America's forgetful West.

I've probably picnicked on the sites of massacres
And they always seemed quite halcyon to me—
So Europe's eastern woods will have some picnickers. . . .

It's beauty's foolproof secret: failed memory
Or, rather, no memory at all;
Though there are other tactics. In the National Gallery,

Van Eyck's seemed almost possible to steal:
You overwhelm by sheer obsessive diligence,
With such exhaustive slavery to detail

That each tiny window in a castle in the distance
Has a bird or cat or flower on its sill;
An infinitesimal pool mirrors the elegance

Of a horseman on a bridge, the flustered sail
Of a fishing boat outfoxed by a reflected gull
With a reflected fish in its reflected bill. . . .

If I were that meticulous, would this be beautiful?
Laura, Lorenzo, and I rode by a river.
If I could depict each willow, reed, and cattail,

Each concentric ripple's modest quiver,
Would I be able to concoct a thing so full
That this cup would finally run over?

Don't take that question seriously. It's rhetorical.
Detail was merely background to Van Eyck
For a virgin or saint or other allegorical

Allusion, probably a kind of gimmick
To divert himself, to keep from going stale,
Commission after commission, from getting slick;

He wanted something pointless, something personal,
Some in-joke only he would be amused by—
Unless it was a kind of secret arsenal

To shore himself against the possibility
That the saint or virgin or angel wouldn't come
(At least over worldly things, you can have mastery),

Or maybe this was how he gained momentum—
One minute a reflected horse, next a saint—
I wonder if he could have dreamed up our museum,

A clearing in a vague, uncharted continent,
Where crowds would gather for an instant to possess
Whatever it was that he sat down to paint. . . .

At the Frick the guard will give you a magnifying glass
To ogle the elaborate commotion
Behind the distracted virgin's grieving face. . . .

But there are other versions of precision—
The explanatory note beside a Chinese scene
(I also hit the Freer that day in Washington)

Said that painters often added poems to fill in
What would otherwise have been an empty sky. . . .
And then there's the current taste for installation

Like the one I caught at the museum in LA,
Where I found myself staring in a garage—
An actual garage—complete with disarray. . . .

You walk into this utterly random hodgepodge
(My first reaction was to crack a joke:
Another piece on loan from the Hermitage?

Then to remember what Amata said, when I first took
Her—at the age of sixty-three—to the Uffizi;
She was standing in front of Giotto's polyptych:

E dicono che l'uomo va avanti?
And they say man is making progress?).
But I got so involved in what there was to see—

The weird headlines, ticket stubs, glass eyes,
Torn calendars, posters, steamy paperbacks—
The Uffizi wasn't mine, but this *was*—

One ticket was even from Utah—unmatched socks,
Boots, ice skates, sandals, tennis shoes,
Jacket covers from discarded books—

Am I making this up? There *were* glass eyes,
And I'm sure there was a ticket stub from Utah,
My own Utah — such a surprise —

But the rest is a blur; I should have stayed,
But I didn't want to have the realization
That, at best, this was the very thing I did —

Amass eccentric bits in one location.
But if I'm right and beauty *is* failed memory,
Then I should have a different revelation:

Namely, that I'm barking up the wrong tree. . . .
Forget the Cohen brothers, Amata, my father-in-law;
Pick a color, any color; pick two or three —

The gold-vermilion gashes in my Utah;
The orange opportunist in its injured stone,
A daredevil acrobat in every flaw:

Arch, butte, mesa, hoodoo, canyon. . . .
I should take my cue from the Colorado —
Where can you find an artist with more ambition,

Tenaciousness, technique, sheer bravado?
Think if you could do that with a pen,
If a voice could have that limitless vibrato. . . .

Give up, it's saying, *look at me, give in.*
Stop typing for a second and feast your eyes;
I thought I came to Italy for inspiration,

But it was escape I was looking for, disguise —
Cultivated hills that you can talk about,
Slim, expurgated skies,

As if that little masquerade could cancel out
Their red-gold secret: sheer, impervious,
Hurtling toward the outer edge of *infinite*

And utterly oblivious to us. . . .
I'm floundering here. I need a rhyme . . .
Some human thing—an Anasazi dwelling place

(Multi-leveled, with ladders you can climb),
Tucked beneath an unsuspecting overhang
In the seemingly unoccupied sublime.

Don't tell me people lived there without a pang
Of self-consciousness, ambition, doubt, desire. . . .
I won't believe they never sang,

Never meant to pitch those ladders higher
Before whatever—whoever? —wiped them out,
Left them at the mercy of my conjecture.

In Italy, at least, you're never in doubt
Of what its lost inhabitants were after:
They'd purify whatever it was, pluck it out,

And rush it onto not-yet-hardened plaster—
And even now, thinking of them, I'm satisfied
(By *now*, I mean in Utah, on a static chair;

You didn't think I wrote all this on that train ride?)—
Frescoes are what I thought this poem was for . . .
How I climbed the scaffolding, stood right beside

What I'd only ever guessed at from the floor.
Believe me, my cup's still running over.
But I don't think I'll say any more,

Not now, anyway; maybe when I'm braver
Or less bewildered, less at a loss;
You have to be—to some degree—a believer

When you get yourself involved in a poem like this;
Not only that there is, somewhere, a listener
Who's moved by what you say, reveal, confess,

But that you actually have a chance against the executioner
Who's trying to wipe you out without a trace. . . .
So why am I acting like an auctioneer

(Who'll give me something, anything, for this?)
And if I feel this way, why not press *delete?*—
It's not as if I've ever actually printed this;

I prefer it, to tell the truth, as bits of light
Or whatever LED is—liquid something or other—
I'll pretend it was an accident, bemoan my fate,

How I'd finally achieved my one *chef-d'oeuvre*
And some desperate type came knocking at the door. . . .
Now all I remember's a damsel with a dulcimer,

Her head dissolving in the damaged air—
Indelible, beneath her sleeve, a bright-blue bridge
Rising from some abyss to stop midair

Between what really happens and the dense mirage
That haunts the magnifying glass, the train stop,
The rumpled keepsakes heaped in a garage,

The gold-stone campanile on a hilltop,
The cliff dwelling's vanished entourage,
The royal harpist with his too-full cup

Showering Emily Dickinson, Hopkins, Coleridge. . . .
Why should I press *delete?* I'd just wind up
Repeating myself. Why not acknowledge

That I can't do any better than this: my cup . . .
My trip, my windfall, my Roman winter foliage,
My Amata, my Laura, my train, my lack of sleep,

My Italian-speaking muses with their rhymed barrage
Of place names, paintings, panoramas, gossip,
My crowded sky's reflected afterimage,

My skyscraper around a tenement, my muted landscape,
My jokey, too self-conscious sabotage,
My father-in-law, my husband, my unsalvageable Europe,
My terza rima poem, my camouflage.

ABOUT THE AUTHOR

Jacqueline Osherow has received fellowships from the John Simon Guggenheim Foundation, the National Endowment for the Arts, and the Ingram Merrill Foundation, and has been awarded the Witter Bynner Prize by the American Academy of Arts and Letters. She has received a number of awards from the Poetry Society of America. Her poems have appeared in many journals and anthologies, including *The New Yorker, Paris Review,* and *Best American Poetry, 1998.* She directs the creative writing program at the University of Utah.